AF559560

Shani Chalisa

Shani Chalisa

Published in Sanskriti Press
Rupa Publications India Pvt. Ltd 2025
161-B/4, Gulmohar House,
Yusuf Sarai Community Centre,
New Delhi 110049

Sales centres:
Bengaluru Chennai
Hyderabad Kolkata Mumbai

P-ISBN: 978-93-7003-624-6
E-ISBN: 978-93-7003-678-9

First impression 2025

10 9 8 7 6 5 4 3 2 1

Printed in India

Contents

Introduction / 7

Chalisa / 11

श्री शनिदेव आरती / 57

Shri Shanidev Aarti / 59

Introduction

Among the many deities in the Hindu pantheon, Shani Dev stands as a powerful and mysterious figure—one who evokes both reverence and reflection. He is the celestial embodiment of the planet Saturn, the lord of karma and justice, and the divine force who ensures that every soul experiences the consequences of its actions. Born to Surya Dev, the radiant Sun God, and Devi Chhaya, his shadow-consort, Shani Dev's presence reminds us of the inescapable law of cause and effect that governs the universe.

Shani Dev is not a god of punishment, as he is often misunderstood, but rather a strict teacher whose lessons are rooted in righteousness and truth. He tests the ego, disciplines the mind, and humbles the proud so that the soul may evolve. His gaze—feared for its power to delay, obstruct, or challenge—is, in truth, a divine glance of correction, meant to realign the devotee with the path of dharma.

The Shani Dev Chalisa invokes the glory and compassion of this just and noble deity. Through each verse, the Chalisa describes his majestic appearance, his divine vehicle, his symbols of power, and his deep connection to the moral order of the cosmos. It honours him not only as a planetary force but as a compassionate guardian who listens to the cries of the sincere-hearted and offers protection to those who surrender to his will.

Reciting the Shani Dev Chalisa is an act of surrender and spiritual discipline. Devotees chant it with faith to ease the influence of Shani's challenging planetary periods, such as Shani Sade Sati or Dhaiya, and to seek his blessings in times of struggle, delay, or injustice. But beyond seeking relief, this hymn is a sacred reminder to live with integrity, patience, humility, and trust in divine timing.

Chalisa

दोहा

जय गणेश गिरिजा सुवन, मंगल करण कृपाल ।
दीनन के दुख दूर करि, कीजै नाथ निहाल ॥
जय जय श्री शनिदेव प्रभु, सुनहु विनय महाराज ।
करहु कृपा हे रवि तनय, राखहु जन की लाज ॥

Jay Ganesh Girija Suvan,
Mangal Karan Kripal.
Deenan ke dukh door kari, kijai Nath Nihal.
Hail Ganesha, son of Parvati, the merciful bringer of auspiciousness.
Remove the sufferings of the humble and bless them, O Lord.

Jay Jay Shri Shanidev Prabhu, Sunahu Vinay Maharaj.
Karahu Kripa he Ravi Tanay, Rakhahu jan ki Laj
Victory to Lord Shani! O great king, please hear my humble praycr.
Grant your grace, O son of the Sun, and protect your devotee's honour.

जयति जयति शनिदेव दयाला ।
करत सदा भक्तन प्रतिपाला ।।
चारि भुजा, तनु श्याम विराजै ।
माथे रतन मुकुट छवि छाजै ।।

Jayati Jayati Shanidev Dayala,
Karat Sada Bhaktan Pratipala.
Chaari Bhuja, Tanu Shyam Virajay
Maathe Ratan Mukut Chavi Chaijay.

Glory, glory to merciful Shanidev, always protecting his devotees.
With four arms and a dark form, a jeweled crown adorns his head.

परम विशाल मनोहर भाला ।
टेढ़ी दृष्टि भृकुटि विकराला ।।
कुण्डल श्रवन चमाचम चमके ।
हिये माल मुक्तन मणि दमके ।।

Param vishal manohar bhala,
tedhi drishti bhrikuti vikarala.
Kundal shravan chamacham chamke,
hiye maal muktan mani damke.

He has a broad, handsome forehead, and
a fierce, slanted gaze.
Shining earrings adorn his ears, and a
garland of pearls glows on his chest.

कर में गदा त्रिशूल कुठारा ।
पल बिच करैं अरिहिं संहारा ।।
पिंगल, कृष्णो, छाया, नन्दन ।
यम, कोणस्थ, रौद्र, दुःख भंजन ।।

Kar mein gada trishool kuthara,
pal bich karain arihin sanhara.
Pingal, Krishno, Chhaya Nandan, Yam,
Konasth, Raudra, Dukh Bhanjan.

He holds a mace, trident, and axe,
destroying enemies in moments.
He is Pingal, Krishna, son of Chhaya,
Yama, Konasth, Raudra, and destroyer of
sorrow.

सौरी, मन्द शनी दश नामा ।
भानु पुत्र पूजहिं सब कामा ।।
जापर प्रभु प्रसन्न हवैं जाहीं ।
रंकहूं राव करैं क्षण माहीं ।।

Sauri, Mand, Shani dash nama,
Bhanu putra pujhin sab kama.
Japar prabhu prasann hawain jahin,
rankahun raav karain kshan maahin.

Known by ten names including Sauri and Mand, the Sun's son fulfills all desires. Whoever pleases Lord Shani, even a pauper becomes a king instantly.

पर्वतहू तृण होइ निहारत ।
तृणहू को पर्वत करि डारत ॥
राज मिलत वन रामहिं दीन्हयो ।
कैकेइहुँ की मति हरि लीन्हयो ॥

Parvatahu trin hoi niharat, trinahu ko parvat kari daarat.
Raj milat van Ramahin dinhayo,
Kaikeyiun ki mati hari linhayo.

He can make mountains appear as grass and grass as great as mountains. He sent Rama to exile though he was about to be crowned, altering Kaikeyi's mind.

वनहुं में मृग कपट दिखाई ।
मातु जानकी गई चुराई ।।
लक्ष्मणिंह शक्ति विकल करिडारा ।
मचिगा दल में हाहाकारा ।।

Vanahun mein mriga kapat dikhai,
Matu Janaki gayi churai.
Lashanahin shakti vikal karidara,
machiga dal mein haahakaara.

A deceptive deer led to Sita's abduction from the forest.
Lakshman was struck and fell unconscious, chaos broke out in the army.

रावण की गति–मति बौराई ।
रामचन्द्र सों बैर बढ़ाई ।।
दियो कीट करि कंचन लंका ।
बजि बजरंग बीर की डंका ।।

Ravan ki gati-mati baurai,
Ramchandra so bair badhai.
Diyo keet kari kanchan Lanka,
baji Bajrang bir ki danka.

Ravana's thoughts turned mad, and he worsened his enmity with Rama. Golden Lanka was reduced to ashes; the drums sounded with Hanuman's victory.

नृप विक्रम पर तुहि पगु धारा ।
चित्र मयूर निगलि गै हारा ।।
हार नौलखा लाग्यो चोरी ।
हाथ पैर डरवायो तोरी ।।

Nrip Vikram par tuhi pagu dhara,
chitra mayur nigli gai haara.
Haar naulakha lagyo chori,
haath pair darvayo tori.

You stepped on King Vikram's life; a painted peacock swallowed his necklace. The valuable necklace was blamed as stolen, and his limbs were shackled.

भारी दशा निकृष्ट दिखायो ।
तेलहिं घर कोल्हू चलवायो ।।
विनय राग दीपक महँ कीन्हयों ।
तब प्रसन्न प्रभु ह्वै सुख दीन्हयों ।।

Bhari dasha nikrisht dikhayo,
telahin ghar kolhu chalvayo.
Vinay raag deepak mah kinyayo, tab
prasann prabhu hvai sukh dinhayo.

A terrible phase befell him; he was made
to operate an oil press.
He sang humble ragas like Deepak;
pleased, the Lord granted him relief.

हरिश्चन्द्र नृप नारि बिकानी ।
आपहुं भरे डोम घर पानी ।।
तैसे नल पर दशा सिरानी ।
भूंजी-मींन कूद गई पानी ।।

Harishchandra nrip nari bikani,
aaphun bhare dom ghar paani.
Taise Nal par dasha sirani, bhoonji-meen
kood gayi paani.

King Harishchandra sold his wife and fetched water in a dom's house. Similar fate struck King Nala; even the fish he roasted jumped back into the water.

श्री शंकरहिं गह्यो जब जाई ।
पार्वती को सती कराई ॥
तनिक विकलोकत ही करि रीसा ।
नभ उड़ि गयो गौरिसुत सीसा ॥

Shri Shankarahin gahyo jab jaai,
Parvati ko sati karai.
Tanik viklokat hi kari reesa,
nabh udi gayo Gaurisut seesa.

When you afflicted Lord Shiva, you
caused Parvati to become a sati.
Just one angry glance made Ganesha's
head fly up into the sky.

पाण्डव पर भै दशा तुम्हारी ।
बची द्रोपदी होति उधारी ।।
कौरव के भी गति मति मारयो ।
युद्ध महाभारत करि डारयो ।।

Pandav par bhai dasha tumhari,
bachi Draupadi hoti udhari.
Kaurav ke bhi gati mati marayo,
yuddh Mahabharat kari darayo.

Your phase came upon the Pandavas;
Draupadi was saved only by divine grace.
You ruined the minds of the Kauravas and
caused the Mahabharata war.

रवि कहँ मुख महँ धरि तत्काला ।
लेकर कूदि परयो पाताला ।।
शेष देव-लखि विनती लाई ।
रवि को मुख ते दियो छुड़ाई ।।

Ravi kahn mukh man dhari tatkala,
lekar koodi parayo patala.
Shesh dev-lakhi vinati laai,
Ravi ko mukh te diyo chhudai.

You once entered the mouth of the Sun
and leapt into the netherworld.
Only after other gods prayed did Sheshnag
release the Sun from your grasp.

वाहन प्रभु के सात सुजाना ।
जग दिग्गज गर्दभ मृग स्वाना ।।
जम्बुक सिह आदि नख धारी ।
सो फल ज्योतिष कहत पुकारी ।।

Vahan prabhu ke saat sujana,
jag diggaj gardabh mriga swana.
Jambuk sih aadi nakh dhaari,
so phal jyotish kahat pukari.

The Lord has seven wise mounts:
elephant, donkey, deer, and dog among them.
Fox, lion, and others arc also his mounts,
whose effects astrologers declare.

गज वाहन लक्ष्मी गृह आवैं ।
हय ते सुख सम्पत्ति उपजावै ।।
गर्दभ हानि करै बहु काजा ।
सिह सिद्धकर राज समाजा ।।

Gaj vahan Lakshmi grih aavai,
hay te sukh sampatti upjavai.
Gardabh haani karai bahu kaja,
sih siddhkar raj samaja.

When he rides the elephant, wealth comes home; on a horse, happiness grows. Donkey brings loss in many tasks; lion grants power and royal success.

जम्बुक बुद्धि नष्ट कर डारै ।
मृग दे कष्ट प्राण संहारै ।।
जब आवहिं स्वान सवारी ।
चोरी आदि होय डर भारी ।।

Jambuk buddhi nasht kar daarai,
mriga de kasht praan sanhaarai.
Jab aavahin swan sawari,
chori aadi hoy dar bhaari.

Fox ruins intellect; deer causes distress and even loss of life.
When he arrives on a dog, thefts and deep fear abound.

तैसहि चारि चरण यह नामा ।
स्वर्ण लौह चाँदी अरु तामा ।।
लौह चरण पर जब प्रभु आवैं ।
धन जन सम्पत्ति नष्ट करावैं ।।

Taisahi chari charan yah nama,
swarn lauh chandi aru tama.
Lauh charan par jab prabhu aavai,
dhan jan sampatti nasht karavai.

Likewise, his four steps are known as
gold, iron, silver, and copper.
When he comes in iron phase, he brings
great loss to people and wealth.

समता ताम्र रजत शुभकारी ।
स्वर्ण सर्वसुख मंगल भारी ।।
जो यह शनि चरित्र नित गावै ।
कबहुं न दशा निकृष्ट सतावै ।।

Samta tamra rajat shubhkaari,
swarn sarvasukh mangal bhaari.
Jo yah Shani charitra nit gaavai,
kabahun na dasha nikrisht sataavai.

Copper and silver bring peace; gold brings all joys and great fortune.
Whoever recites this Shani hymns daily is never tormented by ill phases.

अद्भुत नाथ दिखावैं लीला ।
करैं शत्रु के नशि बलि ढीला ।।
जो पंडित सुयोग्य बुलवाई ।
विधिवत शनि ग्रह शांति कराई ।।

Adbhut Nath dikhavain leela,
karain shatru ke nashi bali dheela.
Jo pandit suyogya bulavai, vidhivat
Shani grah shanti karaai.

Wonderful is the Lord's divine play, which destroys enemies' strength.
Call a learned priest and perform Shani pacification rites as prescribed.

पीपल जल शनि दिवस चढ़ावत ।
दीप दान दै बहु सुख पावत ।।
कहत राम सुन्दर प्रभु दासा ।
शनि सुमिरत सुख होत प्रकाशा ।।

Peepal jal Shani divas chadhavat,
deep daan dai bahu sukh paavat.
Kahat Ram Sundar prabhu daasa,
Shani sumirat sukh hot prakaasha.

Offer water to the Peepal tree on
Saturdays and give lamps for great joy.
Says Ram Sundar, a servant of the Lord—
meditating on Shani brings light and joy.

॥ दोहा ॥

पाठ शनिश्चर देव को, की हों 'भक्त' तैयार ।
करत पाठ चालीस दिन, हो भवसागर पार ॥

Path Shanischara dev ko,
ki hon 'bhakt' taiyaar.
Karat path chalis din,
ho bhavsagar paar.

Those who become true devotees and recite this for forty days,

Shall surely cross the ocean of worldly existence.

।। इति श्री शनि चालीसा ।।

Iti Shri Shani Chalisa

Thus ends the sacred Shani Chalisa.

श्री शनिदेव की आरती

जय जय श्री शनिदेव भक्तन हितकारी ।
सूरज के पुत्र प्रभु छाया महतारी ।।
।। जय जय श्री शनिदेव...।।

श्याम अंग वक्र-दृष्टि चतुर्भुजा धारी ।
नीलांबर धार नाथ गज की असवारी ।।
।। जय जय श्री शनिदेव...।।

क्रीट मुकुट शीश राजित दिपत है लिलारी ।
मुक्तन की माला गले शोभित बलिहारी ।।
।। जय जय श्री शनिदेव...।।

मोदक मिष्ठान पान चढ़त हैं सुपारी ।
लोहा तिल तेल उड़द महिषी अति प्यारी ।।
।। जय जय श्री शनिदेव...।।
।। जय जय श्री शनिदेव...।।

देव दनुज ऋषि मुनि सुमिरत नर नारी ।
विश्वनाथ धरत ध्यान शरण हैं तुम्हारी ।।

जय जय श्री शनि देव भक्तन हितकारी।।
।। जय जय श्री शनिदेव...।।

Shri Shanidev Aarti

Jai Jai Shri Shanidev Bhaktan Hitkaari
Sooraj ke putra Prabhu, Chhaya mahtaari
Jai Jai Shri Shanidev...

Shyaam ang vakra-drishti chaturbhuja dhaari
Neelambar dhaar Naath, gaj ki savaari
Jai Jai Shri Shanidev...

Kirit mukut sheesh raajit, dipat hai lilaari
Muktan ki maala gale shobhit balihari
Jai Jai Shri Shanidev...

Modak mishtaan paan chadhat hain supaari
Loha til tel urad, mahishi ati pyaari
Jai Jai Shri Shanidev...
Jai Jai Shri Shanidev...

Dev danuj rishi muni, sumirat nar naari
Vishwanath dharat dhyaan,
sharan hain tumhaari
Jai Jai Shri Shani Dev Bhaktan Hitkaari
Jai Jai Shri Shanidev...

Shri Shanidev Aarti

Victory, victory to Lord Shani,
benefactor of devotees!
Son of the Sun God, O Lord,
and Chhaya is your mother.
Victory, victory to Lord Shani...

Dark-complexioned, with a crooked gaze,
bearer of four arms,
Clad in blue garments, O Lord,
riding a majestic elephant.
Victory, victory to Lord Shani...

A crown adorns your head,
shining brightly,
A garland of pearls graces your
neck—truly praiseworthy!
Victory, victory to Lord Shani...

Offerings of sweets, betel leaves,
and delicacies are made to you,
Iron, sesame oil, black lentils, and your
beloved buffalo are dear to you.
Victory, victory to Lord Shani...
Victory, victory to Lord Shani...

Gods, demons, sages, monks—all
chant your name,
Even Lord Vishwanath meditates upon

you and seeks your refuge.
Victory, victory to Lord Shani,
benefactor of devotees!
Victory, victory to Lord Shani...